S0-EDB-200

Armadillos, Anteaters, and Sloths

HOW THEY LIVE

Armadillos, Anteaters, and Sloths

HOW THEY LIVE

Jane E. Hartman

Holiday House, New York

Printed in the United States of America

Library of Congress Cataloging in Publication Data

Hartman, Jane E
Armadillos, anteaters, and sloths.

Bibliography: p. 89
Includes index.
SUMMARY: Discusses the three remaining examples of edentates: Armadillos, anteaters, and sloths.
1. Edentata—Juvenile literature. [1. Armadillos. 2. Anteaters. 3. Sloths] I. Title.
QL737.E2H37 599'.31 79-20699
ISBN 0-8234-0400-5

To the memory of Grace and Maude

ACKNOWLEDGMENT

My sincere thanks to Dr. Eleanor E. Storrs, Research Professor at the Division of Comparative Mammalogy and Biochemistry, Medical Research Institute, Florida Institute of Technology at Melbourne, Florida, and to Dr. Bill L. Lasley of the Research Department at the Zoological Society of San Diego, for sharing some of their knowledge and data about current research involving armadillos.

Contents

LEONARD LEE RUE III

The armored armadillo looks like a jumble of different animals with its mule ears, pig eyes, and rat tail.

1
The Curious Edentates

What kind of creature has the eyes of a pig, the tail of a rat, the ears of a mule, and the armored scales of an alligator? If you can solve this riddle, you've recognized one of the edentates—in fact, the only one to be found in the United States: the armadillo.

The edentates are probably the most primitive and unusual mammals found in the New World. Sloths, anteaters, and armadillos are included in this biological order, the Edentata.

The word "edentate" means "toothless," although this description is inaccurate, since only the anteater is truly without teeth. However, the three edentate families are very different from one another, as well as from other mammals, in structure, including teeth or lack of them, appearance, and life styles.

The edentates are primitive animals physically, with the armadillo as the most primitive—little changed over thousands of years. (Anteaters have apparently advanced most of all.) However, their brains have few convolutions and are relatively simple. Other internal organs include parts that were developed and remain unchanged since their early evolution, as well as the more recently developed parts.

Possibly because these animals are extremely sensitive to cold, the edentates have networks of blood vessels called "retia mirabilia," or retes, that allow them to conserve heat. These networks are composed of blood vessels meshed together in such a way that the arteries and veins lie next to each other. In this way, heat flowing with the blood from the trunk of the animal's body is trapped, transferred, and returned by the veins to the trunk rather than going completely to the limbs, where it would be easily lost.

The sloth, for example, suffers when the temperature drops below 26.6° Celsius (80° F), a situation that occurs many nights. The retes help the animal adjust by letting its limbs cool to the outside temperature while keeping its vital organs

AMERICAN MUSEUM OF NATURAL HISTORY

The three-toed sloth, like most edentates, is a warm weather creature, suffering when the temperature drops below 26.6° Celsius.

warm and protected. It takes a sloth two hours to reheat a front leg from 15° Celsius (59° F) to 25° C (77° F).

The principle used here is known as "counter-current exchange," by which a warm stream will lose its heat to a cooler one. In the case of the retes, the warmth in the arterial blood will pass through the tissue walls to the cool venous blood.

Another unusual aspect of the physical structure of sloths, anteaters, and armadillos is that they have extra articulations, or movable parts, between vertebrae in the lumbar region of the back—just above the hips. These additional parts give support to the animal's hips, although armadillos seem to be the only edentates that actually make use of these, which they do when digging. No other living mammals have these extra articulations.

The parts are known as xenarthrales. The edentates are survivors of a biological suborder called Xenarthra, a populous group during the Tertiary period in the earth's history, millions of years ago. At that time the edentates were numerous. There were many different species. As a matter of fact, today there are about 30 fossil forms of edentates, compared to only three living ones.

An Old, Old Family

The ancient edentates came in a variety of forms. The earliest of these, some 60 million years ago, had teeth that lacked enamel, and had a bony armor. In fact, it is assumed that all the early edentate types had armor.

South America was the home of the early edentates. They developed there at a time when that continent was separate from North America. This was during the Tertiary period. Before that the two land masses were connected; the earliest edentate ancestors were from North America.

Several million years ago—no one knows for sure exactly when—many of the South American edentates began to wander. Their travels brought some of them up through Central America to North America. The giant sloths, some the size of elephants, were first. They were followed during the Ice Age by armadillos and the armored glyptodons. These creatures were almost as large as a rhinoceros. Sloths and anteaters, strictly warm-weather creatures, came only as far as Central America.

Today most of these unique animals have disappeared and only the three edentate families remain. These are the armadillos (Dasypodidae), the

SAN DIEGO ZOO

The tamandua is one of several anteater species found in South and Central America.

anteaters (Myrmecophagidae), and the sloths (Bradypodidae). One reason given for their survival when so many others failed is that these animals occupied specialized habitats. This specialization enabled them to avoid the predators and hoofed mammals that invaded their native areas during the Ice Age, wiping out any competing edentates. Of the survivors, only the armadillo—the animal that answers our riddle—is found in the United States. At that, it is found only in warm areas, since this animal, like the rest of its group, cannot live in cold weather.

2
Sloths and How They Live

High in the top of the rain forest, a sloth hung upside down. Its long sickle-shaped claws had a viselike grip on the branch above it. It remained in this position much of the time, resting and eating. Very slowly and deliberately, the straw-colored animal pulled off the leaves and blossoms, using its horny lips, or its claws. Very slowly it inched from one spot to another more promising one, chewing leisurely. Now it would remain motionless for a long period, resting, dozing.

All sloths are slow-moving creatures. In fact, the name "sloth" comes from an Old English term for "slow." Because of its sluggish behavior (or slothfulness!) the animal is also called "lazy man" in parts of South America.

SAN DIEGO ZOO

A sloth spends part of its time hanging upside down high in the trees.

Sloths range in length from 50 to 65 centimeters (about 20 to 25 inches) and weigh from four to nine kilograms (some nine to 20 pounds), depending on their species. Most have dun-colored, long hair that is worn reversed; that is, instead of parting on the back like most animals' fur, the sloth's hair parts on its belly. This peculiarity, one of many, lets rain and moisture run off as the sloth hangs in its topsy-turvy position.

Sloth fur is constructed with two grooves that provide homes for two species of one-celled plants called blue-green algae—Trichophilus and Cyanoderma. As they thrive in the moisture of the sloth's jungle environment, the algae give a greenish cast to its fur coat. However, during periods of drought when almost everything dries out, the algae turn yellow—still providing camouflage for their host. This is a symbiotic relationship, one in which two kinds of organisms, the algae and the sloth, live together with mutual benefit. The algae are not the only ones to benefit from the sloth's fur, however. The rare snout moth, also called the sloth moth, lays her eggs in the sloth's straggly coat. These moths actually live on the algae in the sloth's fur, which prevents the insects from spreading too much.

Protective Fur and Skin

A sloth's fur coat is quite thick. It acts as insulation, protecting the animal from cold and heat. Excessive exposure to unusual heat as well as to extreme cold can kill this mammal. A sloth's coat can vary according to its habitat, too. Hoffmann's sloths *(Choloepus hoffmanni)*, living in the harsh mountainous parts of Panama, have coats quite different in length and in the quality of the fur from similar sloths found in coastal areas.

Besides very thick hair, sloths have extremely tough skins. The hair and skin combine to give the animal a type of protective armor against biting ants and predators on land and in the water.

A sloth's actions also protect it against excessive heat or cold, as do the actions of many other animals. It can ball up tightly in the crotch of a tree to conserve its body heat when the temperature drops. However, oddly enough, cold-sensitive sloths do not shiver, a common muscular reaction to cold weather found in most mammals.

When it is very hot, a sloth stretches out on its hairy back, exposing its belly. It appears that the sloth loses body heat from its less hairy underside. Sloths also pant like dogs, and may even wet their fur if they can find water.

Sloths lack incisors, or cutting teeth, so they use their horny lips or claws for grasping food. They can rip off leaves and hold them in their mouths, eating all the while in a constant process. Sloths get their permanent teeth before they are born. The teeth do not have enamel and apparently grow all the time to compensate for their centers being hollowed out from grinding food.

Conserving Energy

The physiology and anatomy of the sloth are excellent examples of the adaptations made throughout its long evolution. These have allowed it to survive more efficiently in its kind of habitat. Because an inactive animal like the sloth uses much less energy than an active one like a deer, for example, its food requirements are lower. One researcher has said that a sloth absorbs only one-seventh of the food eaten by a young fawn of the same weight.

A sloth is slowly active about four hours of a day, and sleeps or rests the remaining 20 hours. It may do this hanging upside down or sitting. Bradypus, one of the two sloth genera, spends less than 10 per cent of its lifetime in an upside-down position. It is a great sitter, sleeping or resting in the fork of a tree for hours. The slow functioning of the sloth is also an important factor in combating the heat of its habitat.

Sloths have much less skeletal musculature—the muscles used in moving about—than other mammals. In fact, the amount of muscle tissue in the sloth amounts to only 25 per cent of its body weight. That is about half of what is found in other mammals. Muscles are the main heat-producing tissues in the body.

This lack of muscle tissue may also contribute to the very low metabolic rate—the rate at which food is converted to tissue and energy—found among sloths. The sloth metabolic rate is about 36 to 66 per cent that of other mammals that are approximately their size. Low metabolism means low body heat, and this is a characteristic of slow mammals. It may also be a way of conserving energy. A sloth's body temperature may vary between 24° and 33° C (75° and 91° F). It is also influenced by the surrounding, or ambient, temperature. For comparison, a dog or cat may have a body temperature of about 38° to 39° C (100° to 102° F), a little higher than that of a human.

Possibly because of its life style, some of the sloth's internal organs are located differently from those found in other mammals. The liver, for example, has turned nearly halfway to the rear. Its spleen and pancreas are on the opposite side from where they are located in other mammals.

Another unique feature of the sloth family is a very efficient bladder; they can go for a week without urinating. Their bladder is unusually large and can be stretched a great deal by its liquid content. The animals appear to get all their necessary water from the vegetation upon which they feed, or by lapping up dewdrops on the leaves. Sloths also defecate only occasionally.

NEW YORK ZOOLOGICAL SOCIETY

NATIONAL ZOOLOGICAL PARK

Bradypus, the three-toed sloth, left, has three claws on all four feet. Choloepus, the two-toed sloth, above, has two long sickle-shaped claws on its front feet and three on its back feet.

Two Toes and Three Toes

There are a number of differences between the two sloth genera, Bradypus, the three-toed sloth, and Choloepus, the two-toed sloth. They can be told apart most easily by counting their front toes (sometimes, though rarely, called fingers). Both types have three toes on their rear feet. Another and equally obvious difference is in the tail. The three-toed sloth has a stubby tail, while the two-toed has none at all. In addition, the two genera really do not look alike. The two-toed has a doggish muzzle with small eyes, while the three-toed appears to have a more human-looking head, with large round eyes that look straight forward.

Three-toed sloths also have unusual stomachs. They are somewhat like those of ruminants, plant-eating, cud-chewing animals, such as cows or deer. The right and left halves are divided into a number of compartments that apparently have different functions. This may be the result of this sloth's very specialized diet. The intestines are short, indicating that the food remains in the stomach for most of the digestive process.

The Bradypus sloths also have 30 ribs and nine neck vertebrae, the largest number of such vertebrae found in mammals. Possibly because of this, long-necked Bradypus has neck and head movements similar only to an owl's. The animal can swivel its head 180°, as can owls, and can look forward while its body faces backward. Two-toed sloths, or Choloepus, have only six or seven neck vertebrae. They have 48 ribs, however.

A Leafy Life

As we have said, most of a sloth's life is spent in the trees, sometimes hanging upside down or resting on a branch. Even mating occurs in the trees, and so does birth. After a pregnancy of about five to six months (or six to seven in some cases) the female sloth gives birth to her single infant. During this process she frequently hangs by her arms, with her legs dangling earthward. Then the young is born, headfirst, usually without being covered by embryonic membranes. To keep it from falling she grabs the infant with a claw as it emerges from her body; and the infant helps too, by clutching its mother's fur as soon as it is able. It takes from 15 to 30 minutes for an infant to be born. After that it stays with its mother until it is ready to go on its own.

There are differences too between the sloth genera in their treatment of the young, which will be examined more closely in the next chapter.

Almost everything a sloth does takes place in trees; the exceptions are their occasional defecation, which may occur in special areas on the ground, and some of their traveling. In the early part of the rainy season they may migrate; the reason for this is unknown. At that time they even cross large rivers and go into totally unfamiliar areas. Sloths are good swimmers, either on their abdomens or on their backs, where they do an effective "lazy man's" backstroke.

On the ground, sloths are most awkward. They have to drag themselves almost painfully across the earth. They travel about three to four and a half meters (some 10 to 15 feet) per minute on the ground, while they can move approximately 30 meters (about 100 feet) per minute in the trees.

When a sloth is on the ground, or in the sturdy lower branches of a tree, it is most vulnerable to predators. Its main enemies (aside from humans, who hunt it as food) include large snakes like the anaconda, harpy eagles, ocelots, and caimans, a type of American crocodilian. All of these predators usually catch a sloth when it is helpless on the ground, or unable to climb to higher or weaker branches. Frequently, however, a sloth cannot be dislodged easily from its perch by a predator. Because of its thick hide and coat as well as a tight-fitting rib cage, an eagle, for example, is some-

SAN DIEGO ZOO

Sloths draw themselves across the ground awkwardly.

times not able to mortally wound the sloth with its sharp talons. As additional protection, sloths have remarkably quick and efficient healing powers and survive injuries that would kill many other creatures.

3
More About Sloths

There is some difference of opinion among biologists about the number of sloth species, but in this book we will think of them as having five species. They are found in the forested regions of Central and South America. This is appropriate considering that sloths with their slow body processes must have warm weather.

The two-toed sloth, or unau, as it is called locally, is found in northern Brazil, Bolivia, Equador, Guyana, Venezuela, Panama, and Nicaragua. It can range in length from 60 to 64 centimeters (about 23 to 25 inches) and it weighs about nine kilograms (almost 20 pounds). These sloths are the most studied and the easiest to keep in captivity,

SAN DIEGO ZOO

Hoffman's two-toed sloth is rarer than the common two-toed sloth.

NEW YORK ZOOLOGICAL SOCIETY

The common two-toed sloth can have either 24 or 25 chest vertebrae—the greatest number found in any mammal.

because their diet is not so specialized as that of their three-toed relatives. They are also much more active and agile than the three-toed sloth and will put up quite a battle if captured. Their two long toes, the second and third, have sickle-like claws that can be about the length of a human adult's little finger. The soles of their feet are hairless and very calloused from clutching branches.

There are probably two species of two-toed sloths: Hoffmann's *(Choloepus hoffmanni)* and the common or South American *(C. didactylus).* The common sloth has 25 or 26 thoracic (chest) vertebrae—the greatest number found in any mammalian species. Of the two species of two-toed sloth, Hoffmann's is the rarer.

These well studied two-toed sloths have a very sharp sense of taste, are probably nearsighted, and seem to have poor hearing. This latter apparent inability, however, may be part of the sloth's desire to be inconspicuous, since sloths that are in captivity as house pets hear very well. One scientist reported that sloths even seem to enjoy music. The sloth also has a well developed sense of smell. Bradypus, for example, uses this sense to locate and test its food plants.

The family life of the two-toed sloth differs from that of the three-toed. The newborn Choloepus is independent at about nine months. Before that it is cared for by its mother. For about four weeks it stays hidden in her long hair. Then it begins to venture out on brief exploratory trips, learning about its leafy surroundings and tasting some of its mother's food. Eventually it is ready

A baby two-toed sloth stays hidden in its mother's hair for about four weeks.

AMERICAN MUSEUM OF NATURAL HISTORY

to go out on its own. When that time comes, the mother sloth chases her young whenever it approaches her.

The Curious Ais

The three-toed sloth is also called an ai, from the wailing sound it occasionally emits. It can be found on river shores and along the edges of forests from Argentina to Honduras. It is a skilled swimmer as well as climber. The chief diet of the ai includes flowers, fruits, and leaves of the cecropia tree, which is a tropical relative of the mulberry. Therefore the animal lives within a limited area and is more difficult to keep in captivity. It has been found that the ants that live in the cecropia tree are also eaten by the sloth as it munches the leaves. The nutrients provided by the ants are apparently necessary to this sloth's health.

The ais are generally much smaller than the two-toed species. Because of their long, stiff hairs, ais appear to have manes. In addition, their hair styles can run anywhere from bangs to a crew cut.

In color, the two sloth genera differ. The ais may be gray-brown with bright spots. Males are more colorful than females, and also sport a large leaflike patch on their backs. The ais have small, round heads, somewhat like a human baby's. Their necks are long. They have a small mouth and no noticeable ears, because these are buried in their fur.

Sloth arms are longer than their back legs. Like its two-toed relative, the ai has three toes on the back foot, with long claws. These can be used in defense of itself, although ais are usually very docile. In addition, their actions are so slow, they do not do much harm. This sloth also has its soles covered with hair, unlike the unau.

There are three sloth species within this genus. The South American three-toed sloth *(Bradypus tridactylus)* is the most common. *B. cuculliger,* from Guyana and Bolivia, has exceptionally long hair on its head and shoulders, giving it a sheep dog look. The third species *(B. torquatus),* from northwest Brazil and Peru, is called the necklace sloth. It has a black band across its neck and shoulders from which it gets its name.

As was mentioned, the name "ai" was given to Bradypus because of its two-syllabled, high-pitched cry. This is heard often during the mating season in March and April, as well as when a sloth is hurt, or when mother and young are separated. Apparently these sloths have no real vocal cords, only rudimentary tissues. Their shrill cry comes through their nasal passages. On the other hand, the unau has regular vocal cords like those found in other mammals. Aside from its few vocalizations, a sloth's life apparently shows no real communication behavior.

The family life of the ai is similar to that of the unau in that the animal remains alone; this is especially true of ais. After a brief mating, and birth of the young, the mother rears her infant. However, the ai mother apparently is not so careful of the youngster as is the unau; she often forgets her young one. Fortunately, the young ai is completely self-reliant at birth. This youngster is called "fast Peter" *("Perico ligeiro")* by the natives of its homeland. This is because it is so much quicker than an adult sloth.

During the daily routine of eating, sleeping, and even mating, sloths appear to show no emotions; their faces are often said to be expressionless. People who have kept them as pets, however, consider the animals to have a very friendly look, and they are apparently far from stupid, as early observers reported. If it is attacked, a sloth will often fight, using its teeth and rear claws; and as we have seen, a young one cries if separated from its mother. In such a case the mother will be moved to look for it, though on occasion it is distracted and forgets to finish the search. On the whole, the animals' slowness and deliberation

usually act in their favor, protecting them from predators by their very inconspicuousness.

Strategic Defense

Not being noticed is the sloth's greatest defense. All of its life style is keyed to this way of living. It is a master of camouflage. Balled up in a tree crotch, or hanging from a branch, a sloth looks like a termite nest or a knot on a tree. The moths and algae mentioned earlier as making their homes in the sloth's coat help the animal blend into its surroundings and be all but invisible. The sloth's arms and legs are straight, and when it lets them hang they look like branches.

Basically, all its behavior avoids attracting attention. It does not go where there is trouble. It can outwait most predators because its needs are fewer than those of other animals. It eliminates not only infrequently but also in an inconspicuous way. It may defecate during a rainstorm when its whereabouts won't be noticed and the sound of its feces dropping will be masked by the sound of the rains. Otherwise, it may climb down

The mother ai is sometimes forgetful of her young one. Fortunately an ai is completely self-reliant at birth. SAN DIEGO ZOO

a tree, dig a hole, defecate, and cover its traces by burying its wastes. A sloth appears to have no odor. It also has endless patience to match its extremely slow movement. When it wants to change its position and go to another area, it times its progress through the trees to a period when the breezes are stirring the leaves. Then it won't be noticeable by either sound or sight as it moves. A sloth can remain in one spot for a very long time, however. Altogether, it is an expert at surviving.

4
Anteaters and How They Live

The giant anteater ripped open the termite nest, using a slashing blow of its right front foot. Its long claws tore through the hard surface of the nest until the big animal could stick its long tubular nose into the opening. Digging deeper and deeper into the insect nest, it finally located the center of the colony. Then it pushed its sticky wormlike tongue out, working it back and forth rapidly, bringing back into its mouth the many insects that stuck to its tongue. These were ground up by the horny projections on the roof of the anteater's mouth, on the insides of its cheeks and in its stomach.

After eating its fill—a giant anteater can consume 30,000 insects every day—the long-haired animal wandered off through the high grasses. It looked for a sheltered spot at the base of a tree, and having found one, dug itself a hole. In this it lay on its side, head between forepaws, and slept for a while. The anteater's body in its temporary resting spot was just level with the ground. Its natural straw-colored form blended into its surroundings so well it couldn't be noticed easily.

The giant anteater is the only toothless edentate; it has no trace of teeth at all. Its two relatives, however, the tamandua and the silky anteater, do have vague remainders of them—what biologists call vestigial teeth. This indicates that at one time in their long evolution these animals had fully developed teeth, which essentially disappeared as their diets became more specialized.

There are three genera among the anteaters. Each has one species. They range in size from about 240 centimeters (about eight feet) for a fully grown giant anteater, including its tail, to some 34 centimeters (about 13 inches), including the tail, for the smallest, the silky anteater. Their weight can vary from 35 kilograms (some 77 pounds) to as little as 500 grams (a little over a pound).

Some smaller anteaters can use their tails, somewhat like certain monkeys, to hold things. However, anteater tails differ. The giant anteater

AMERICAN MUSEUM OF NATURAL HISTORY

The giant anteater is the only edentate that has no trace of teeth at all.

has a very long plumy tail that has scales under all its long hair. The others have thin tails that may have some fur on them, particularly near the base.

A Really Strange-Looking Beast

Anteaters look like no other animal. They have long tubelike snouts that appear to be extensions of their necks. These taper to a pointy mouth. Through this small opening an anteater's tongue, which resembles a ribbon, can flick out and back, picking up many insects at a time and carrying them into the animal's mouth.

The tongue of the giant anteater can be 60 centimeters (over 23 inches) long and move out and in as much as 160 times a minute. Anteaters have tremendous amounts of saliva, in their case a particularly sticky substance that is secreted on the tongue. An anteater's salivary glands are able to produce more saliva than those of any other mammal. These glands are huge, extending as far as the animal's breastbone.

From the mouth the saliva-covered insects are passed to the stomach. Most insects that are still in one piece are ground up by the muscle action of the stomach, aided by the horny lining of this organ. In addition, little stones and sand have been found in anteaters' stomachs. These apparently help in the grinding process.

An anteater's sense of smell is highly developed. It helps the animals locate food, and also to sense enemies in time to escape. In addition it has exceptional hearing. In fact, the source of a sound as far as five miles away can be pinpointed by an anteater.

Although the greater part of anteaters' diet con-

SAN DIEGO ZOO

An anteater's tongue can be as long as 60 centimeters and move in and out as much as 160 times a minute.

sists of insects like termites, ants, and their larvae, the animals will also eat berries and worms. They usually get any moisture they need from their food, or by licking dew or raindrops from vegetation. Anteaters can also swim well. However, unlike many large wild animals, they do not go to streams to drink.

Like sloths, these edentates are well endowed with long, sharp claws. They use these to dig out termites and ants, as well as to defend themselves if the need arises. Most anteaters are docile and use their claws only to protect themselves when threatened. However, an anteater's hug, like a bear's hug, is well known as something to be avoided. When threatened, anteaters of both the giant and the tamandua species will sit up on their haunches like a bear and extend their arms, grasping and hugging anything that gets within range. Getting free of this is very difficult, and both dogs and humans have been fatally injured by a giant anteater's hug. The animal also slashes with its front feet, its strong claws ripping whatever they touch.

Basing their conclusion on the structure of the brain, biologists say that anteaters are the most highly developed of the edentates living today.

5
More About Anteaters

Anteaters are versatile creatures. They can lead their lives entirely on the ground, like the giant anteater, or in the trees part of the time, like the tamandua, or collared anteater. But that's not all: the third member of the family, the two-toed, or silky, anteater, is exclusively a tree-dweller.

The giant anteater *(Myrmecophaga tridactyla)* is the only species in its genus. It is about the height of a large sheepdog, and, as mentioned, may grow to about eight feet in length. It has long, stiff, straw-colored hair that plumes out on its lengthy, very bushy tail. Its color is mainly dark brown with bands of white and black on its head and front legs, giving the effect of dark gray. In addi-

SAN DIEGO ZOO

The giant anteater is about the height of a large sheepdog and may grow to about eight feet in length.

tion, it has a black triangle running back from its throat. The anteater also has a very long mane that goes from its back to join its tail. They are strange-looking creatures indeed.

The nomadic giant anteater prefers open savanna or grasslands for its wanderings. It can be found from Costa Rica to northern Argentina.

Usually it is docile in temperament. However, if it is attacked it will defend itself viciously, using its sharp claws. Its main predators are the jaguar and cougar, but these cats are careful to remain out of range of the anteater's front legs when it sits up to defend itself.

Because of its digging habits, this giant animal can lay waste to large areas of ground. One scientist reported seeing an entire wooded area showing signs of the giant anteater's "destructive habits."

Mates and Young

At certain times of the year, probably spring and fall, the giant anteaters seek their mates. After a six-month gestation period, a single infant is born. A short time after its birth, the young anteater is able to climb up onto its mother's back, where it is carried about for quite a long period of time. At around four weeks of age, however, the youngster is able to run about on the ground. It stays very close to its mother at first, gradually extending its explorations as it gets older.

For two years the young anteater remains with its mother. Then it becomes fully independent and goes off on its own. As a youngster it is very well camouflaged. For example, when a young giant anteater pushes close to its mother it can hardly be seen, its color blends so well with hers. This is important, as young anteaters, like many other wild animal young, are very vulnerable to predators.

The giant anteater is a diurnal, or day-living, animal. When not napping, it moves almost constantly along the ground, sniffing out insect nests.

A Collared Anteater

The second genus of the anteater family, and the second in size, is the collared anteater, or tamandua *(Tamandua tetradactyla),* found from Mexico to Paraguay, a larger range than either of its relatives. It may weigh as much as five kilograms (about 11 pounds). This animal can be terrestrial, or ground-living, like the giant anteater, and sleeps most of the day. It is also at home in trees, climbing about in search of tree termite nests. The tamandua seems to prefer the forest edges, and tree-filled grasslands. It can be found in other types of environment too, such as built-up areas and treeless plains, but these are distinctly not what it prefers. The tamandua climbs slowly, using its long tail as a brace when it breaks up termite nests in the trees with its sharp claws.

RON GARRISON/SAN DIEGO ZOO

The collared anteater, or tamandua, is the second largest in the family. It may weigh as much as five kilograms.

Unlike the giant anteater, the tamandua is a short-haired creature, the covering being thick and bristly. Its color ranges from orange-beige to brown with dark markings on some subspecies. It has a ratlike tail with some fur. Also, the tamandua lacks the long tubular snout found on the giant anteater.

When it is frightened it stands up on its hind legs and grabs anything it can reach. The tamandua will also roll over on its back so it can use all four of its feet for defense if it needs to.

This species is nicknamed "Dominis vobiscum," because it resembles a priest at the altar when it stands upright with its arms outstretched. The tamandua has another nickname given by the human residents of its domain. It is called "stinker of the forest," because of a very unpleasant smell the animal gives off when aroused or excited.

The single young tamandua is usually born in the spring, and like its giant relative is carried about by its mother for a long period. However, the young tamanduas are colored differently from the adults and are easier to spot. The young can be light or orange or even blackish in color.

A Midget

The third species of anteater is the silky, or two-toed *(Cyclopes didactylus).* These are very small indeed compared to the giant species and weigh only about 500 grams (a bit over a pound).

RON GARRISON/SAN DIEGO ZOO

The tamandua is as much at home in the trees as it is on the ground. It uses its prehensile tail much like the small silky anteater does. The latter, however, lives in trees exclusively.

They live in the trees in the hottest parts of Brazil. The silky uses its prehensile tail the way some species of monkeys do, as it makes its way carefully through the forest trees.

The color of this squirrel-like anteater can range from red-brown to a golden yellow. Its hair is short and soft, as its name suggests. The silky has the largest mouth of all its relatives, and a different-shaped forefoot, useful for grasping, perhaps because of its arboreal life style.

Silky anteaters, like tamanduas, sleep most of the day rolled up in the crotch of a tree or in a tree hole. They forage at night. The silky has sharp claws with which it opens tree termite nests, and a long tail that helps to balance it as it uses its front feet to get at the insects.

Like the tamandua and the giant anteater, the silky has one young at a time. However, both silky parents care for and feed the youngster. Sometimes the father carries the young one about on his back, a job done exclusively by the female in the other anteater genera.

These little anteaters are the most difficult to keep in captivity. They are considered to be rare. However, they are extremely difficult to see in their leafy homes, and this may give a false impression as to their numbers in any area.

6
Armadillos and How They Live

The strange armored creature wandered clumsily along the side of the road. Every so often it changed direction and continued its seemingly aimless wandering. Its narrow, scaly head with mulelike ears was just off the ground, its nose sniffing furiously. Suddenly it stopped and began rooting in the loose dirt with its nose until it located what it was digging for: a worm. Promptly it ate the creature, then began its search again, going off in a different direction.

Sounds of dogs barking and baying came close, startling the animal. It started to dig. Holding its breath so dust would not get into its air passageways, the armadillo dug rapidly with its claws.

SAN DIEGO ZOO

Like all armadillos, the seven-banded are master diggers and can use this ability as a method of escape.

And then it was gone, disappearing into the earth just as the first of the hounds appeared. The dogs circled about confused, sniffing the trail. Soon they gave up. The master digger had done its disappearing act again.

The armadillo's first line of defense is to escape, and it can do this by digging in less time than it takes to describe it. Probably because of this ability to dig, the creature is called in Mississippi a "grave digger." It is also known as the "poor man's pig" and "groundhog" (a word reserved mainly for the woodchuck) by some people because this odd animal is in some ways like a hog. The armadillo's vocal sounds are usually "grunts." It roots in the ground for food, and even tastes a bit like pork when cooked. Of course the armadillo's tough, scaly hide is more like some lizards' skin. However, it is neither pig nor reptile; it is the only armored edentate left in the world today. In fact, the word "armadillo" comes from the Spanish and means "armor."

An armadillo's armor plate is something like a turtle's, only much more flexible. It has a leathery piece protecting its shoulders, and another over its rear. Even the tail is covered with bony plates. Between the two plates are bands that are quite flexible. These allow the animal to roll up into a ball. Only its underparts are really vulnerable. When an armadillo is threatened and cannot escape by digging, it rolls up into a tight ball. Many a predator has been frustrated into giving up trying to get through the armadillo's spherical defense.

Not only do most species of this edentate have thick, horny scales, they have body hair as well. In the adults of some species this hair can be abundant.

Teeth and Food

Like the sloth, the armadillo has teeth. However, their number depends upon the particular species. The nine-banded for example, has 32 teeth —16 molars in the rear portion of each jaw—while the giant armadillo has almost 100, more than any other mammal. An armadillo's teeth are not fanglike or sharp. They are rudimentary molars, cylindrical in shape with open areas of pulp (the sensitive tissue in the middle of a tooth). Roots and enamel are lacking. Because of these features, the teeth grow continuously.

Armadillos eat a variety of things in the wild. About 75 per cent of the animal's diet consists of insects. Another 15 per cent is made up of animal material such as worms, carrion, small mammals, reptiles, birds, and eggs. The remaining 10 per cent consists of vegetable matter such as roots. Chewing roots and other hard material is necessary for the health of the animal's teeth and mouth. Zoos have found this out when captive armadillos' teeth grew too long on a soft diet,

If an armadillo is threatened and cannot escape by digging, it rolls up into a tight ball, as did the nine-banded one at top and the three-banded one below. TOP: LEONARD LEE RUE III. BOTTOM: AMERICAN MUSEUM OF NATURAL HISTORY

causing mouth injuries. Hard food causes the teeth to stay worn down normally.

Of all the 21 species, only the giant armadillo *(Priodontes giganteus)* has a specialized diet. This consists of ants and termites. Though the giant has many teeth, they are smaller than those of other armadillos and well suited to its diet.

Like the anteater, the armadillo has sticky saliva and lots of it. Its tongue has little projections rather like warts that, along with the saliva, help trap insects. An armadillo's sense of taste, however, is rather weak, for they have few taste buds. On the other hand, its sense of smell is superb. The nine-banded armadillo, for example, can detect worms and insects as deep as 20 centimeters (almost eight inches) in the ground.

An armadillo's body temperature is around 32° C (90° F). However, experiments have shown that if the surrounding, or ambient, temperature falls to eleven degrees C, an armadillo's body temperature can fall three degrees in four hours. Though it is a warm-blooded animal, it has a temperature situation similar to that of a cold-blooded one: its body heat is directly affected by the outside temperature. It is an animal that cannot survive long in continuing frost or even intermittently cold weather because it cannot keep warm enough for its body to function.

Wandering by Foot and Cattle Car

Because their bodies are so sensitive to outside temperatures, armadillos stick to tropical areas, on the whole, much like the other edentates. However, there is one exception—the nine-banded species, which has migrated north from Mexico into semitropical parts of the United States. It is the only edentate to do so. Its migration to the north is controlled more or less by local temperatures and the availability of suitable insects.

These armored creatures are found from Texas across to Florida and in some fringe areas. In Florida it is said they have now spread to cover one third of the state. In 1979 some were known to have appeared as far north as southeastern Kansas and southwestern Missouri.

According to tales that have been passed around, and may or may not be true, the first armadillos, a pair, were introduced to Florida by a sailor during World War I. The sailor brought the animals from Texas, but they somehow got away near Hialeah. During the 1920s wild armadillos were seen in that general area. In 1924 several other armadillos escaped from a zoo during a storm near Cocoa, Florida. Others got away from a circus, and the Florida takeover by ar-

INTERIOR—SPORT FISHERIES AND WILDLIFE/LUTHER C. GOLDMAN

The nine-banded armadillo has migrated north in the United States. This one was photographed in the San Antonio area of Texas along the Guadalupe River.

madillos was well under way. They have also traveled east from Texas and Mexican-border areas in cattle cars. It appears that they got off with the cattle at stations along the way.

It would seem that humans have helped the armadillo's spread, in the United States at least.

The animals are very fond of many human crops such as peanuts, melons, and tomatoes, and these have enticed them into new areas. The clearing of fields has helped too; the animal loves cut-over areas and thrives under these conditions. In some ways the armadillo helps humans, too. It eats beetles that destroy cane fields, as well as many other insect pests that harm human crops. Unfortunately, armadillos no longer have natural enemies to control their numbers, thanks to our indiscriminate killing of wolves, coyotes, bears, and wildcats. So the armadillo can and does reproduce without any danger except for human gunners, dogs, and cars. Many of these armored edentates are killed on the highways.

7
More About Armadillos

The armadillo family, the Dasypodidae, has more members than either the sloths or the anteaters. Except for the nine-banded armadillo, all are residents of Central and South America. In size they can range from 12 to 100 centimeters (about 5 to 39 inches) in length and weigh from 90 grams to 50 kilograms (about three ounces to 110 pounds).

An important group of armadillos are members of the Dasypus genus. These are small to medium-sized animals, colored from a dark brown to a yellow beige. Their body armor is quite pliable and has anywhere from six to eleven bands. Their tails are as long as their bodies and taper to a point.

Like a strange mixture of animals all put together in one, the armadillos have small, piglike eyes, big ears something like a mule's, and a long snout. These armadillos also have long legs and are fast runners. In fact, they can outrun a human over short distances.

Their claws can be as long as 3.5 centimeters. They use these for opening nests of insects and for digging. This genus is spread from Argentina to Texas as well as through parts of the southern United States.

Many Bands and Few Bands

The nine-banded armadillo is most familiar to us. Besides being the only armadillo living free in the United States, it is the most studied. This species usually has nine bands but can have as many as eleven or as few as eight. They have no hair on their armor, unlike some other species. The nine-banded armadillo has four teats and bears quadruplets from one egg in 120 days. This unusual phenomenon, which will be discussed at length in the next chapter, makes this species a fascinating animal for study. It also allows the species to populate an area in a relatively short period, particularly if the quadruplets are all females. The young nine-banded armadillos stay

SAN DIEGO ZOO

Nine-banded armadillo youngsters stay in their nest for four to six weeks.

in the nest about four to six weeks. Then they go about with their mother looking for food.

Most armadillos can swim, but the nine-banded *(D. novemcinctus)* seems to be the expert. It uses an effective method to cross wide rivers as well as get successfully through flash floods, a hazard that is common in much of its habitat: it sucks in enough air to inflate its stomach and intestines. This supplies a buoyancy that keeps the animal afloat. However, it dog-paddles efficiently too, and for short distances may even walk along the bottom of the waterway. The air system of the nine-banded is well adapted for swimming, and also for digging in dusty places, for it can hold its breath for as long as six minutes.

The largest species in this genus is found in Surinam and parts of Equador and Peru. It is named Kappler's armadillo *(Dasypus kappleri),* and has an extra toe on each of its front feet.

The seven-banded armadillo *(D. septemcinctus)* is sparsely scattered within its range. In many ways it resembles the nine-banded species. However, it carries its unborn young longer and is known to produce four, eight, or even twelve offspring. A very rare member of this group is quite hairy all over, and is sometimes appropriately called the hairy armadillo *(D. pilosus).*

The three-banded armadillos make up the sec-

LEONARD LEE RUE III

When a nine-banded armadillo digs in dusty places, it can hold its breath for as long as six minutes.

ond genus, Tolypeutes. They are especially known for rolling up into a very tight ball. Because of this characteristic as well as their color, the two species are called *bolita,* meaning "little ball," and *tatu naranja,* or "orange armadillo." *Tatu* generally means "armadillo" among the residents of the areas where they are found in South America.

The two species are found in open areas from Guyana to Argentina. They are medium-sized and can be as long as 45 centimeters, with a tail about nine centimeters long. Contrasted with the nine-banded group, these armadillos have tough armor with two to four rings, or bands. Their ears are short, not mulish like their relatives'. However, their legs are long. The females of this group carries her young from five to six months and usually bears only one youngster.

An Armadillo Can Be Cute

The three-banded armadillo *(Tolypeutes tricinctus)* has been described by one scientist who stud-

When you compare the seven-banded with the nine-banded armadillos, can you find any differences in their physical appearance? SAN DIEGO ZOO

ied them in the wild as "decidedly the cutest . . . it runs through the dried grass with its back arched, sniffing about and scraping a bit. . . ." Its first attempt at escape is to flee, but failing that it rolls into a tight ball, after which it can be unrolled only with great effort and strength. This is an effective defense against many of its natural enemies such as foxes and wolves, but has no effect on human hunters. They like to roast *tatu* in its shell. This small armadillo is more day-minded than the others, often foraging during the sunny hours. It has also been kept successfully in zoos.

The second species in this group is *T. matacus.* It has two to four bands and four front toes and five rear ones. The three-banded has five in both front and rear.

The largest of the armadillos is the giant armadillo *(Priodontes giganteus).* It can weigh as much as 50 kilograms. This large species is yellow-brown to dark brown and has very little hair on its body. Its armor is wide and flat, covering its tail as well as its body. Its big ears are rolled in cylindrical fashion. In spite of its size, which might cause one to think it clumsy, the giant armadillo is an efficient digger. Termites make up most of its diet. It digs huge excavations in its search for insects. In fact, one person described a tunnel made by *P. giganteus* as large enough for a man to crawl through.

This species is nocturnal for the most part. It also seems to keep away from people and built-up areas. Because of its tremendous size it can do a lot of damage to agricultural plantings, in which case it can often end up dead. The giant armadillo's meat is not as tasty as that of some other species, so it usually is not hunted for that reason. However, there is evidence that this unusual animal is disappearing. The destruction of its habitat in the jungles of Brazil, and the spread of housing is causing it to become scarce. This development, of course, is affecting many other wild animals as well.

The giant apparently does not adjust readily to captivity either, judging by one specimen brought to New York some time ago. It fell and fatally injured itself as it climbed about its cage, probably looking for an escape route.

Other Giants . . .

The eleven-banded armadillo *(Cabassous unicinctus)* belongs to the giant armadillo group; there are three others. These animals dig long holes into termite nests. Some of these have been as far as five meters underground.

The last of the large armadillos include the six-

NEW YORK ZOOLOGICAL SOCIETY

Six-banded armadillos are unique because they have incisor teeth. Note the hair on this one.

banded and the fairy armadillo, or pichiciago. The six-banded can be yellow to white, with much broader and flatter armor than that of other armadillos. They also have a two-month gestation period, twice yearly. After that time two youngsters are generally born. The six-banded are said to be the best diggers of all.

There are three species in the six-banded genus. *Euphractus sexcinctus,* commonly called the six-banded armadillo, is the northerner in its South American range. The hairy is found farther south. This animal *(E. villosus)* is the true hairy armadillo, and the most prevalent in Argentina. The pigmy armadillo is found even further south. This small armadillo *(E. pichiy)* can weigh one kilogram and reach 35 centimeters in total length, although some are a bit larger.

The six-banded and the hairy armadillos are unique in that they they have incisor teeth. The animals are plentiful within their range and, be-

The true hairy armadillo, a six-banded species, is the most prevalent armadillo in Argentina.

NEW YORK ZOOLOGICAL SOCIETY

cause of their numbers alone, can ruin fields. They also dig holes that horses can step into, with disastrous results. Therefore these armadillos are hunted by gauchos, the South American cowboys of the pampas. The six-banded and the hairy armadillos generally feed at night, although they do go out during the day too.

. . . *and a Fairy*

The fairy armadillo may be the most specialized of the entire armadillo family. There are two genera with one species each. Because of their underground ways these armadillos have been compared to moles. The lesser pichiciago *(Chlamyphorus truncatus)* weighs about 90 grams. It does not have the hard armor most of its relatives have. In fact, this small armadillo has silky skin under its armor. There are 23 to 25 bands. Its ears are simply folds of skin. It has short legs, but its front legs are quite powerful because of its tunneling habits.

The greater pichiciago *(Burmeisteria retusa)* has tougher armor. It has 24 bands, which are fused to the body, while those of its near relative are loosely attached. This is a rare species discovered about 100 years ago.

AMERICAN MUSEUM OF NATURAL HISTORY

Compare this minute 90-gram fairy armadillo rolled into a defensive ball with the nine-banded one on page 56. Note the silken fur on the fairy armadillo.

One anatomical feature that is different in the Pichiciago group is the pelvic plate, which has fused with the spinal column and pelvis. This anchored armor protects the animals in their underground tunnels. The pelvic plate is set almost vertically, giving the animal's body a chopped-off appearance.

The pichiciago also has a tuft of white hairs on its rear end. This gave rise to its Spanish nickname, "Juan Calado" (John Rear). Its chief diet consists of ants and insect larvae. The pichiciago rarely goes above ground, spending most of its life in its tunnels.

8
Armadillos in Research

Of all the edentates, the armadillo has been the most useful to science. The nine-banded armadillo, readily found in parts of the United States, has been helpful in several ways in biomedical research. For example, the use of this animal in the work of Dr. Eleanor E. Storrs resulted in a long needed breakthrough in the battle against leprosy.

This ailment, also called Hansen's disease, is an ancient scourge that still inflicts misery on about 15,000,000 people around the globe. Some 3000 Americans are victims of this disfiguring disease. Because of armadillos' susceptibility to leprosy, it is now possible for the first time to try to develop a vaccine to prevent it, and a program has been established by the World Health Organization to achieve this goal.

There are a number of reasons why the armadillo is suitable as an experimental animal in biomedical research. As we already know, the nine-banded armadillo, the species most frequently used, is found easily in parts of the United States. It is also common throughout the rest of its large range. The animal is economical to keep, costing about 37 cents a day. It is also relatively docile, and can be handled with ease. However, there are more important reasons why armadillos make good research animals.

Temperatures and Reproduction

Armadillos have low body temperatures. The temperature of the nine-banded ranges from about 30° to 36° C, depending on the surrounding temperature. Low body heat is most important in leprosy research because leprosy occurs in the cooler parts of the body, such as the skin, fingers, toes, and nose. In fact, this was a main reason the armadillo was chosen in this field of research.

The armadillo is a comparatively long-lived animal with a life span of 10 to 15 years or even longer. Leprosy requires a number of years to

SAN DIEGO ZOO

The nine-banded armadillo baby is being weighed so that growth records can be kept.

develop after innoculation with the leprosy bacillus, *Mycobacterium leprae,* so any animal used for the study of leprosy and other slowly developing diseases must have a long life span.

Probably the major reason the nine-banded armadillo is an attractive prospect for biomedical research lies in its reproductive peculiarities. Unfortunately, the nine-banded species so far has not bred well in captivity. This difficult breeding situation is being studied by a research team at the San Diego Zoo. At this point it appears that the problem rests with the captive female. The male's reproductive functioning seems to be unaffected by its confinement. However, once they have become accustomed to captivity, pregnant females usually will bear and rear their young.

After a gestation period (the time it takes for the young to develop within the mother) of nine months (including a period of three months when the egg, although fertilized, is not developing) the nine-banded armadillo almost always has quadruplets. These four are produced from the same egg, or ovum. In addition, these quadruplets are always all males, or all females.

Identical/Not Identical

The seven-banded armadillo, a much less common but related species from South America,

SAN DIEGO ZOO

One of the reasons armadillos are used in biomedical research is their susceptibility to human diseases such as leprosy and typhus.

may produce four, eight or 12 young. However, it is not clear if these come from a single fertilized ovum.

It was long assumed that any two or more animals coming from the same egg were necessarily identical in every way, because it was thought that the genes in the egg's nucleus were the only things that determined hereditary traits. But the nine-banded armadillo offspring, though they come from a single egg, are *not* necessarily identical. They are alike on the whole, but research has shown that they can differ in various ways, as in their reactions to such things as drugs. Their immune responses also can differ. In one study, skin grafts were made within a set of quadruplets. Reactions were not identical, although they were not as varied as between unrelated sets. Graft tissues were not always compatible—chemically suited to the host tissue—and this resulted in the grafted skin being rejected. This is an immune response by the body to a foreign material—in general, the same kind of reaction the body shows when it fights off disease bacteria.

Leprosy and Other Diseases

In her leprosy research, Dr. Eleanor E. Storrs successfully infected armadillos with *Mycobacterium leprae.* The nine-banded species developed serious leprosy in the lepromatous form, the more serious of the two forms existing, that in time yielded large amounts of the infected tissue. Today this is purified and used in the preparation of a skin test that will make it possible to measure a patient's condition and the progress of the disease. The testing will also allow health officials to gauge the amount of leprosy in the world. This valuable material can be produced in the large quantities needed because of the nine-banded armadillo's susceptibility to leprosy. Armadillo strains are being developed in the laboratory to provide "banks" of infected tissue for this purpose. It also appears that, in their wild habitat, nine-banded armadillos contract a leprosylike disease.

There are a number of other areas in which the armadillo with its unique physiological characteristics is helping in human research. Work is being done in organ and tissue transplantation and the study of possible immune reactions, using sets of armadillo quadruplets. The animals have also been found to be highly susceptible to a number of human diseases besides leprosy. Several of these, not all, are tropical. Among them are typhus, schistosomiasis, trichinosis, and relapsing fever.

Because of their susceptibility and reproductive characteristics, armadillos are being used in the study of birth defects. This work includes the study of the effects on the unborn of certain environmental agents such as insecticides and drugs given to pregnant women. There are some similarities in the way the unborn young of the nine-banded armadillo develop and the way a human fetus, or unborn child, develops. This has

RON GARRISON/SAN DIEGO ZOO

Because of its reproductive peculiarities, the nine-banded armadillo is used in embryological research.

led to the use of armadillos in embryological research, particularly in the area of twin, triplet, and quadruplet births. One result of this work might be the development of a drug that would prevent multiple births, or even one that could predictably cause them.

Finally, there are still many things about the

armadillo itself that are not fully understood. Therefore the animal is the subject of study, argument, and speculation among biologists with a special interest in these curious edentates.

Glossary

adaptation: Helpful modification of an organism, through evolution, that fits it better to environmental changes.

ai: The three-toed sloth.

algae: Simple plants that lack true roots, stems, and leaves; some are one-celled, some large seaweeds; most are aquatic.

ambient: Surrounding.

arboreal: Tree-dwelling.

articulations: Movable parts or joints.

cecropia tree: Cecropia lyratiloba, a moderately tall tree with a strange shape and bare branches.

cervical: Pertaining to the neck area.

defecate: To eliminate intestinal wastes.

diurnal: Day-living.

embryo: The earliest stages in the development of an organism, before it has assumed its distinctive shape.

embryological: Dealing with the origin, structure, and development of an embryo.

evolution: The process by which living things change during long periods of time.

fetus: The unborn organism in the later stages of its development.

genus: (pl., genera) A biological grouping of plants or animals ranking next above species and just below family (or sometimes subfamily).

gestation: The period of pregnancy.

graft: A piece of living tissue transplanted to another organism, or to a different spot on the original organism.

habitat: Living area.

incisors: Front teeth adapted for cutting, and for grasping food.

lepromatous: One of two types of leprosy, in which patient resistance to the disease is very weak and the disease spreads widely. Tuberculoid leprosy is a milder form.

metabolism: Body processes that make energy, tissues, and secretions.

nocturnal: Night-living.

ovum: A female reproductive cell, or egg, that when fertilized by a male cell develops into a new organism. The egg we know as food is such a cell accompanied by a large mass of protein to nourish it.

pelvic: Pertaining to the pelvis, the skeletal part that joins the hind limbs to the trunk in a four-legged animal, or the legs to the trunk of the body in two legged animals like humans.

physiological: Pertaining to the processes and functions of living animals and plants, and to the science dealing with them.

predator: An animal that catches other animals for food.

prehensile: Adapted for grasping, such as the tails of some monkeys.

relapsing fever: An acute infectious disease caused by certain spirochetes that are transmitted by lice and ticks.

retia mirabilia: Networks of blood vessels that help an animal conserve body heat.

ruminant: A cud-chewing ungulate, such as a cow, that has a stomach with four separate compartments.

schistosomiasis: A tropical blood disease caused by a parasite that invades the body.

terrestrial: Ground-living.

tertiary: Pertaining to the earlier of two geologic periods in the Cenozoic Era of earth history—the time when mammals, birds, and insects became dominant.

thoracic: Pertaining to the chest, or thorax area.

trichinosis: A disease caused by a parasitic nematode worm; usually contracted by eating poorly cooked pork or other meat.

unau: The two-toed sloth.

vaccine: Any immunizing preparation that can be introduced in the body. It contains viruses or bacteria, usually killed or weakened.

vestigial: Pertaining to a trace or visible sign of a bodily part or organ that remains from one more fully developed in an earlier stage.

xenarthra: A biological suborder of the Tertiary period; ancestors of the edentates.

xenarthrales: Extra articulations found in the edentates.

Suggested Reading

Books

L. S. Brown, *Animals in Motion* (Dover Publications, N.Y., 1957)

M. Goffart, *Function and Form in the Sloth* (Pergamon Press, N.Y., 1971)

John Hoke, *Discovering the World of the Three-toed Sloth,* (Franklin Watts, N.Y., 1976)

Alice Hopf, *Biography of an Armadillo* (Putnam, N.Y., 1976)

Herman Tirler, *A Sloth in the Family* (Walker, N.Y., 1967)

Herbert S. Zim, *Armored Animals* (Morrow, N.Y., 1971)

Magazine Articles

Barbara J. Culliton, "64 Armadillos Threaten a Theory," *Science News,* Nov. 30, 1968

Mary S. Haverstock, "Meet the Armored Spoof," *National Wildlife,* Dec. 1971

David Lampe, "Unmoved and Unloving, the Armadillo Blunders On," *National Wildlife,* Feb. 1977

W. E. Lundy, "The Upside-Down Animal," *Natural History,* vol. 61, 1952

Bill Vogt, "Easy Does It," *International Wildlife,* March-April 1979 (sloths)

G. Causey Whittow, "Night Shift for Sloths and Other Sluggards," *Natural History,* vol. 86, 1977

Index